Little Sweet Twons Lite

INYOURHEAD

Copyright © 2022 INYOURHEAD

Todos los derechos reservados.

ISBN: 9798404759129

DEDICATORY

The following book was created so that you have a lot of time to devote your effort and, above all, the love of your art. Stop to contemplate every little detail, the stories hidden in each page. And if you are a kitten lover, you will see scenes in all their scenes where they interact with their environment or simply, they sleep.WITH A COPY OF EACH DRAWING TO CUT, GIVE OR SIMPLY PROVE AGAIN WITH OTHER COLORS OR MATERIALS.Without further ado, feel free to choose your colors, tones and your adventurous spirit to paint the following pages, enjoy it!

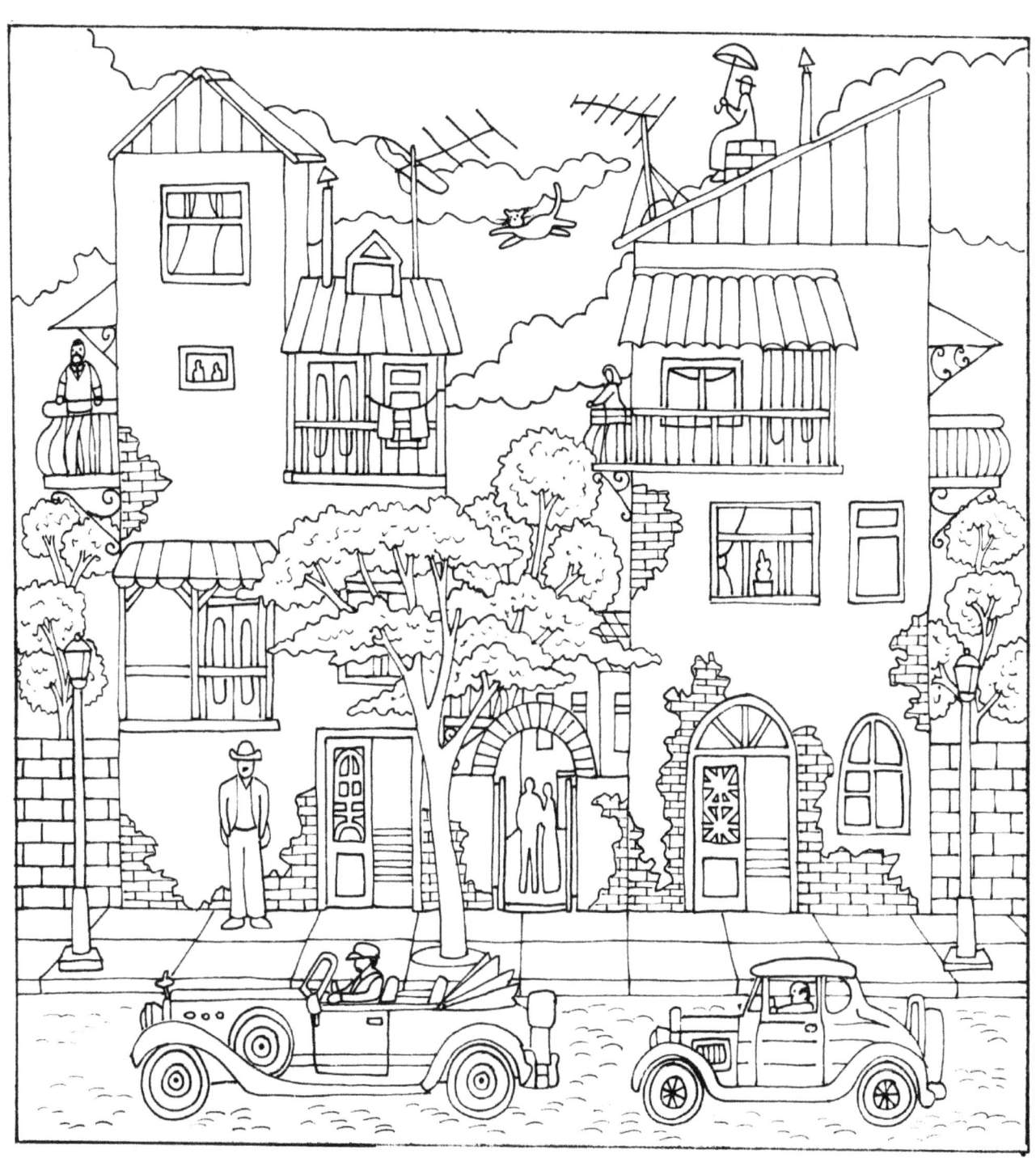

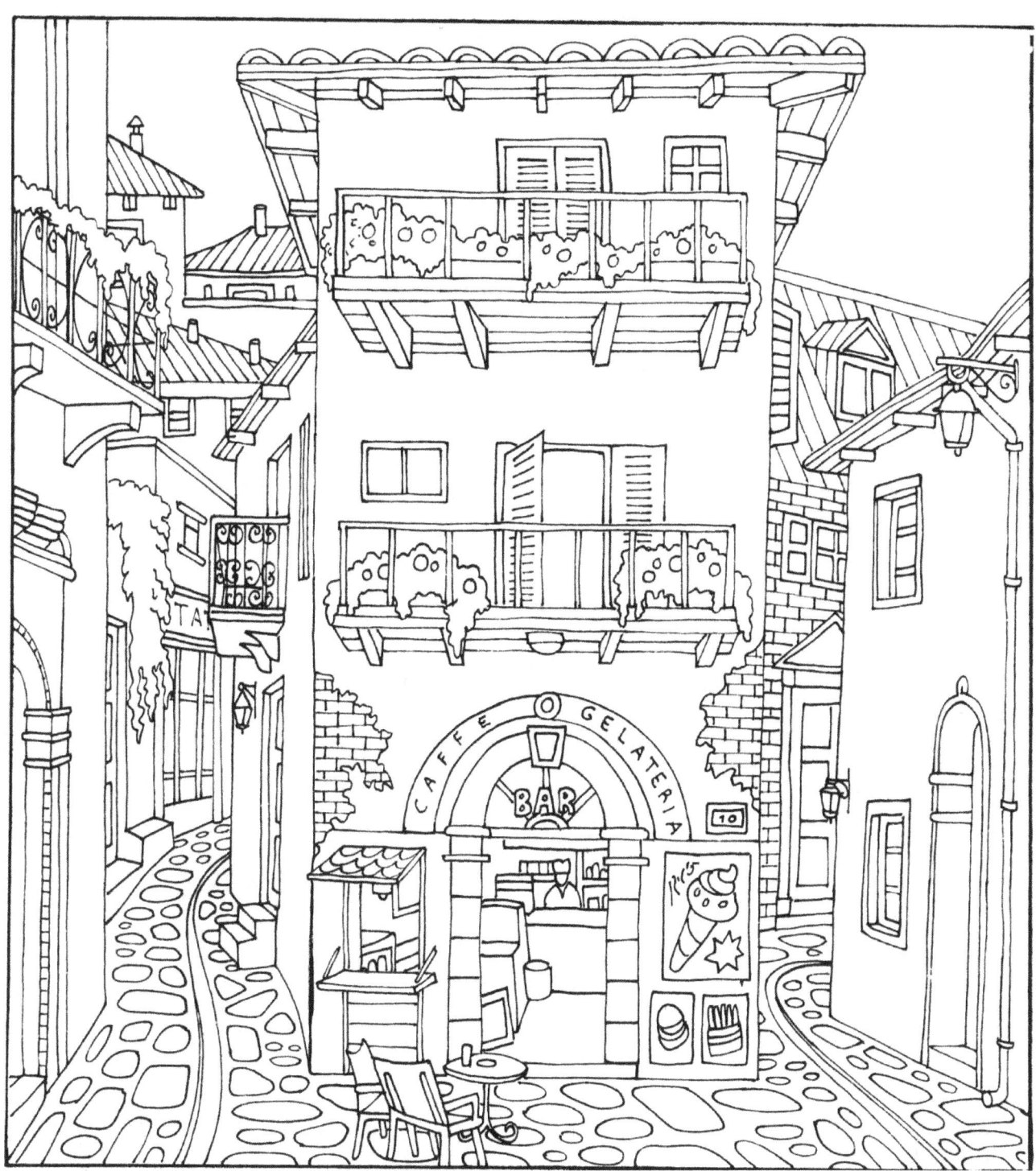

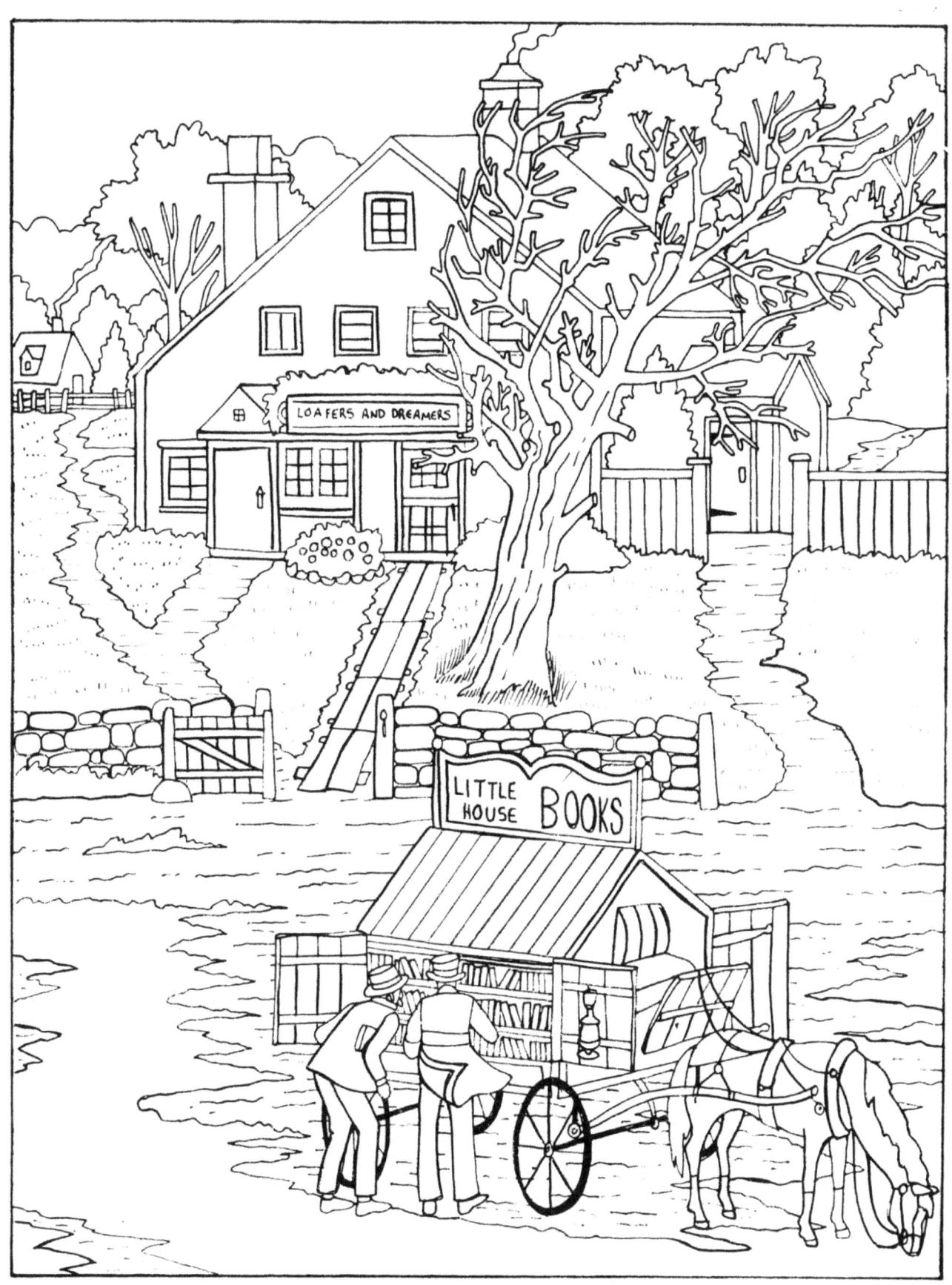

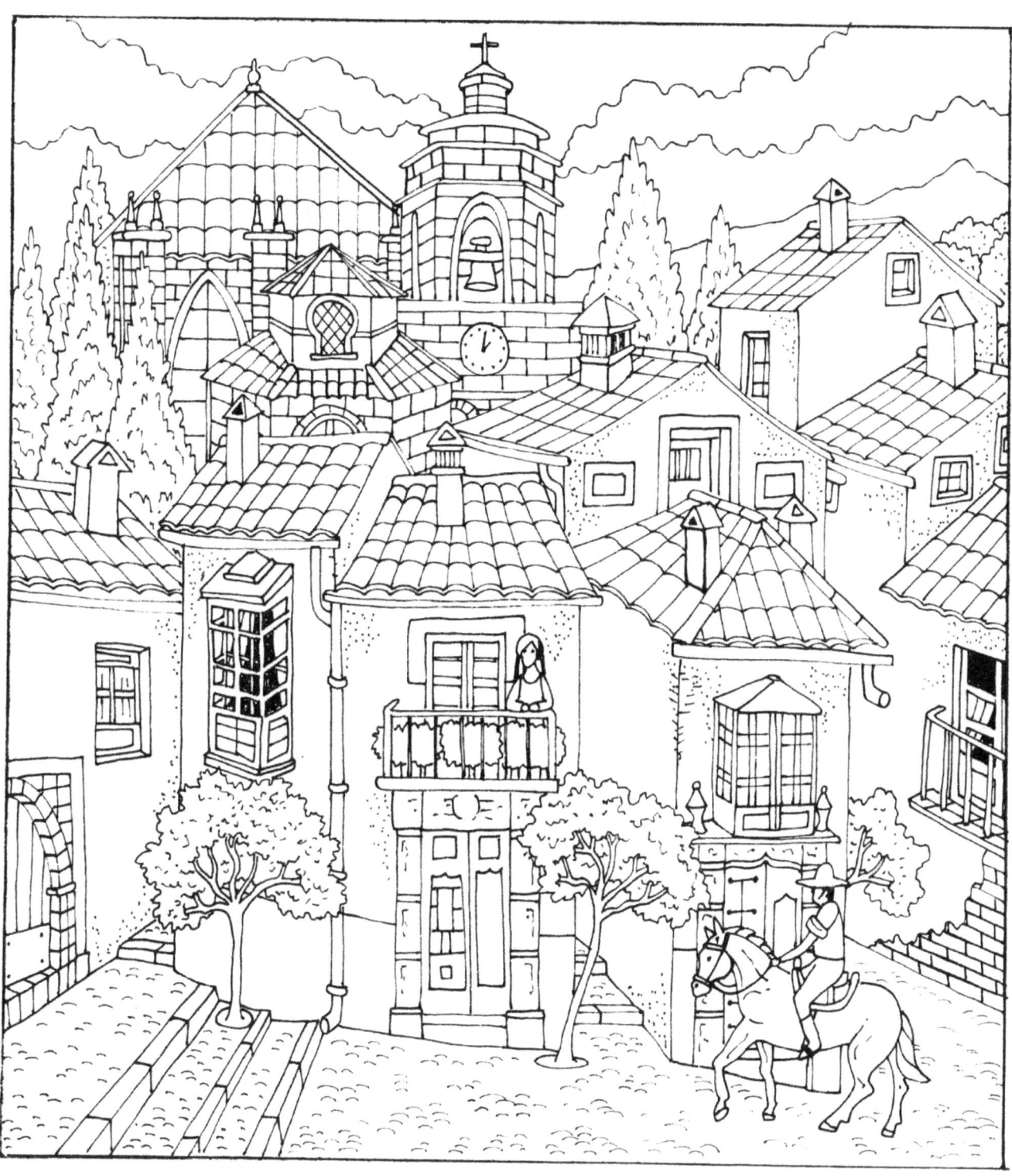

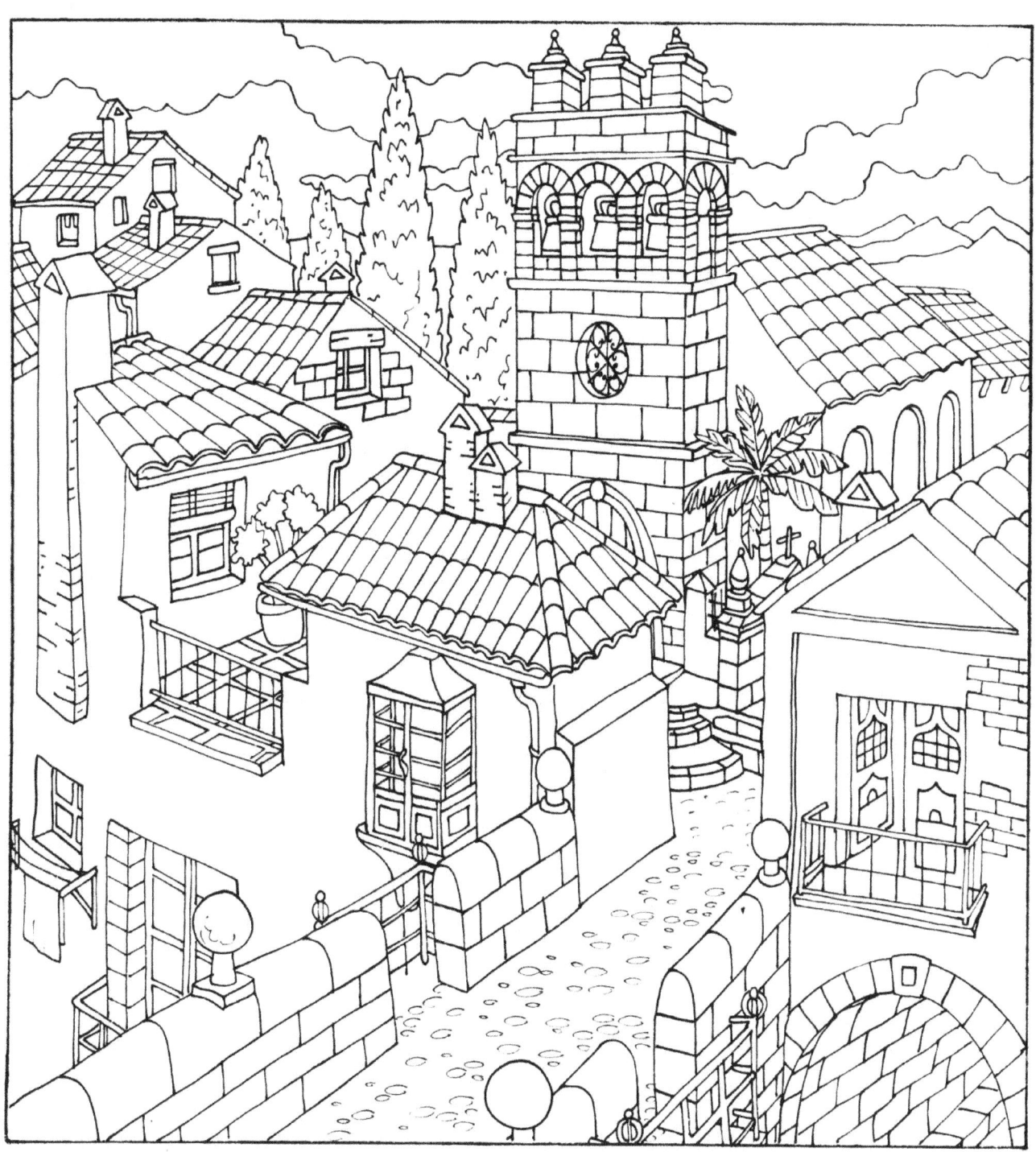

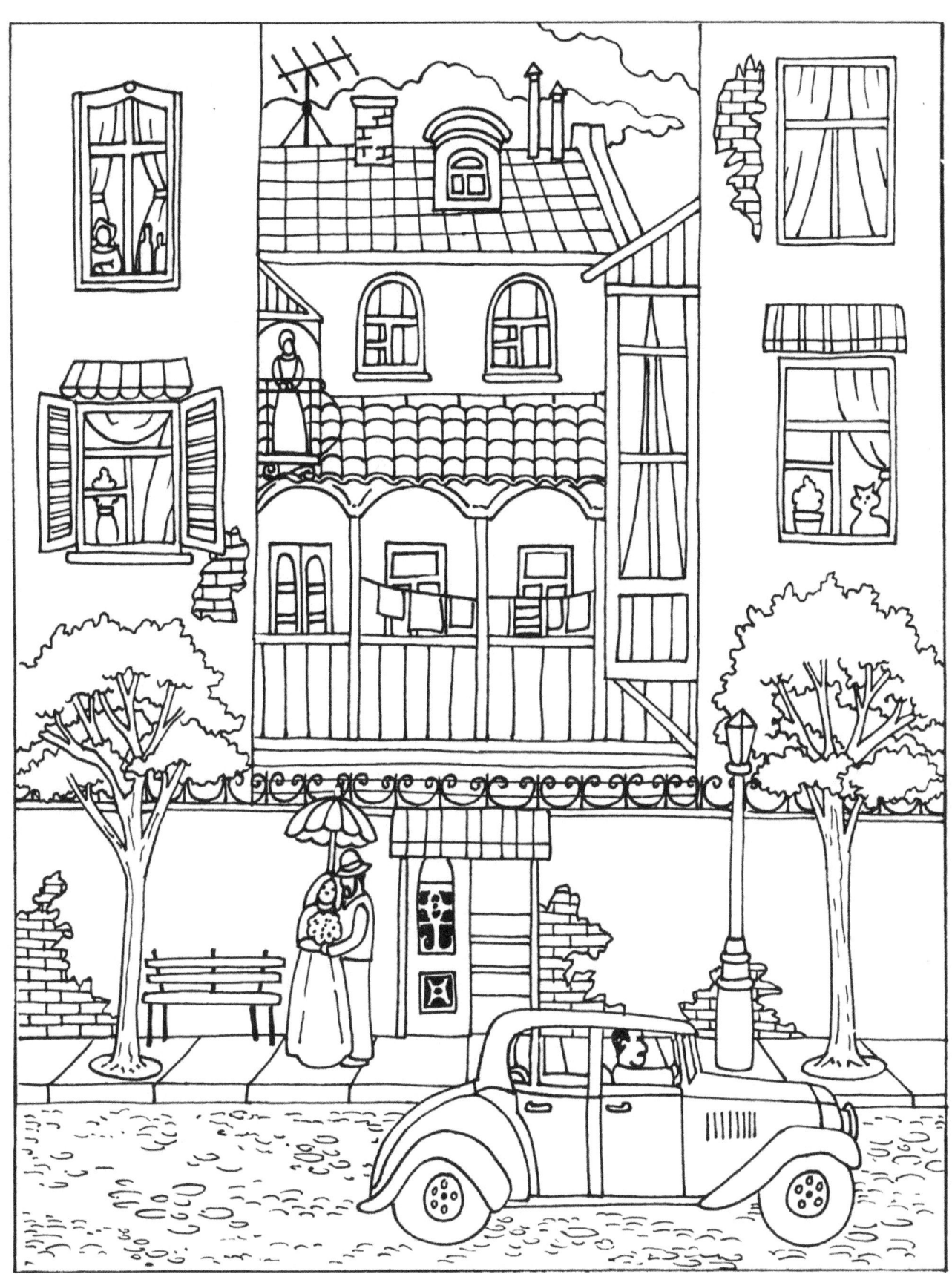

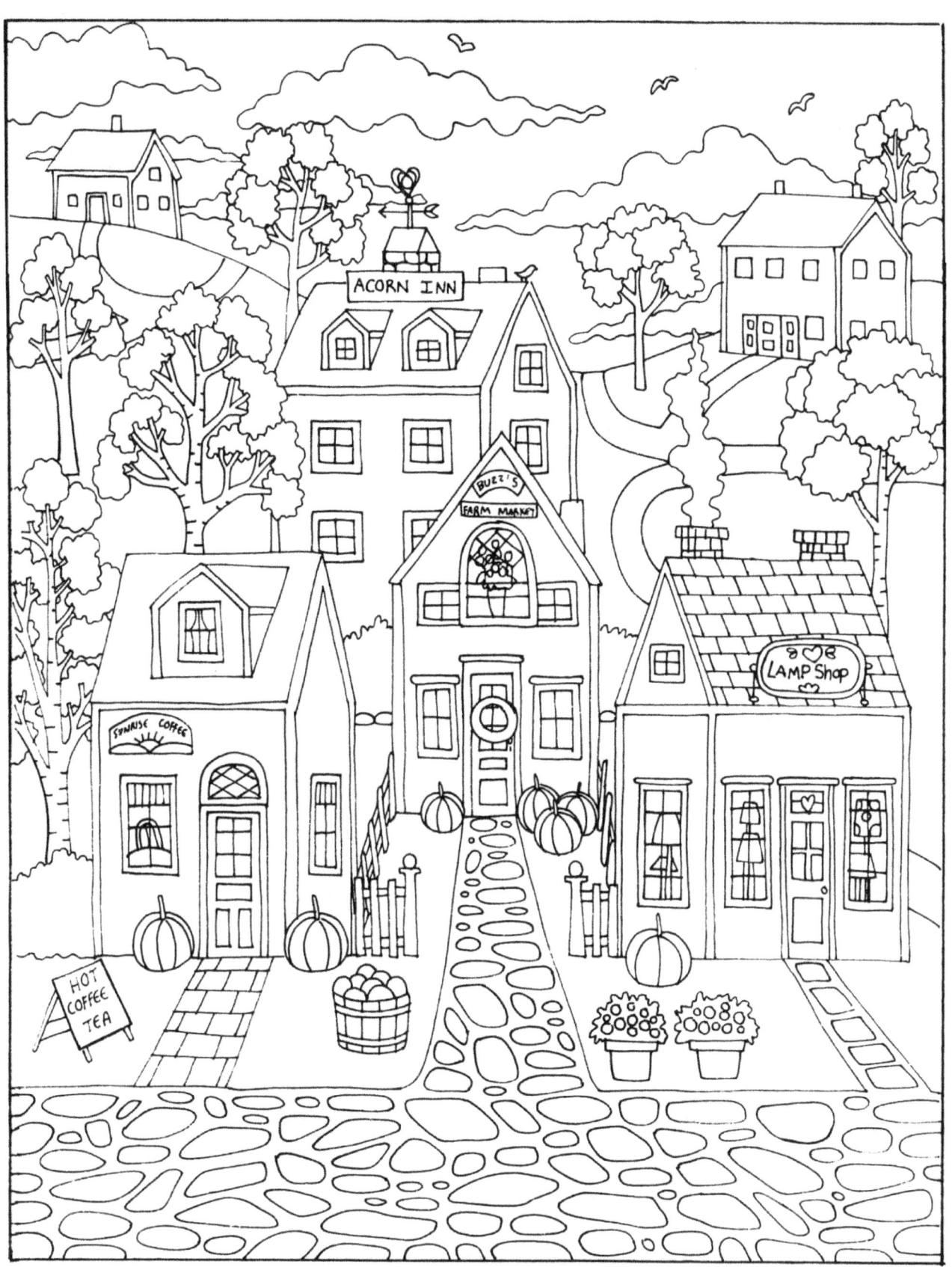

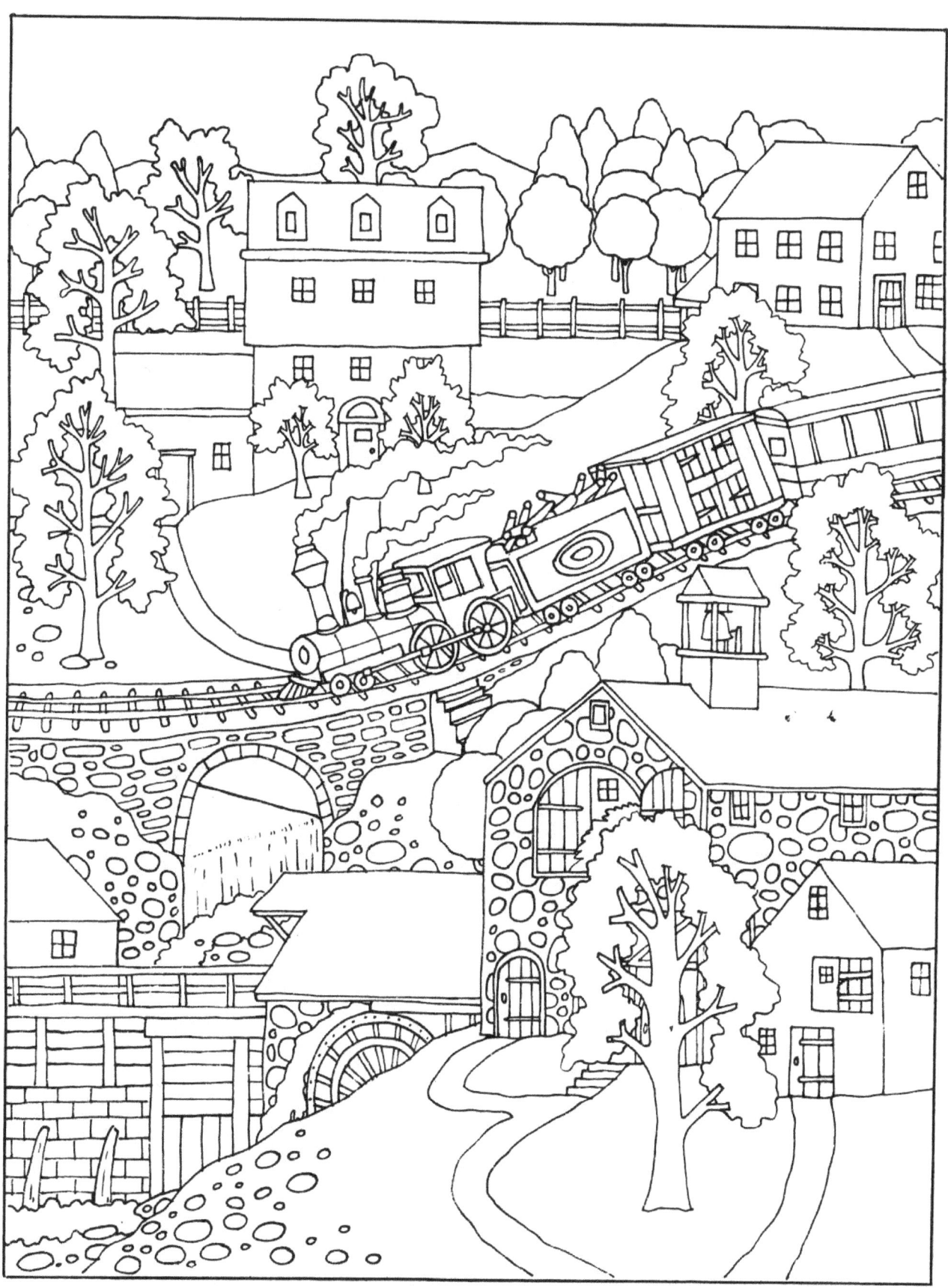

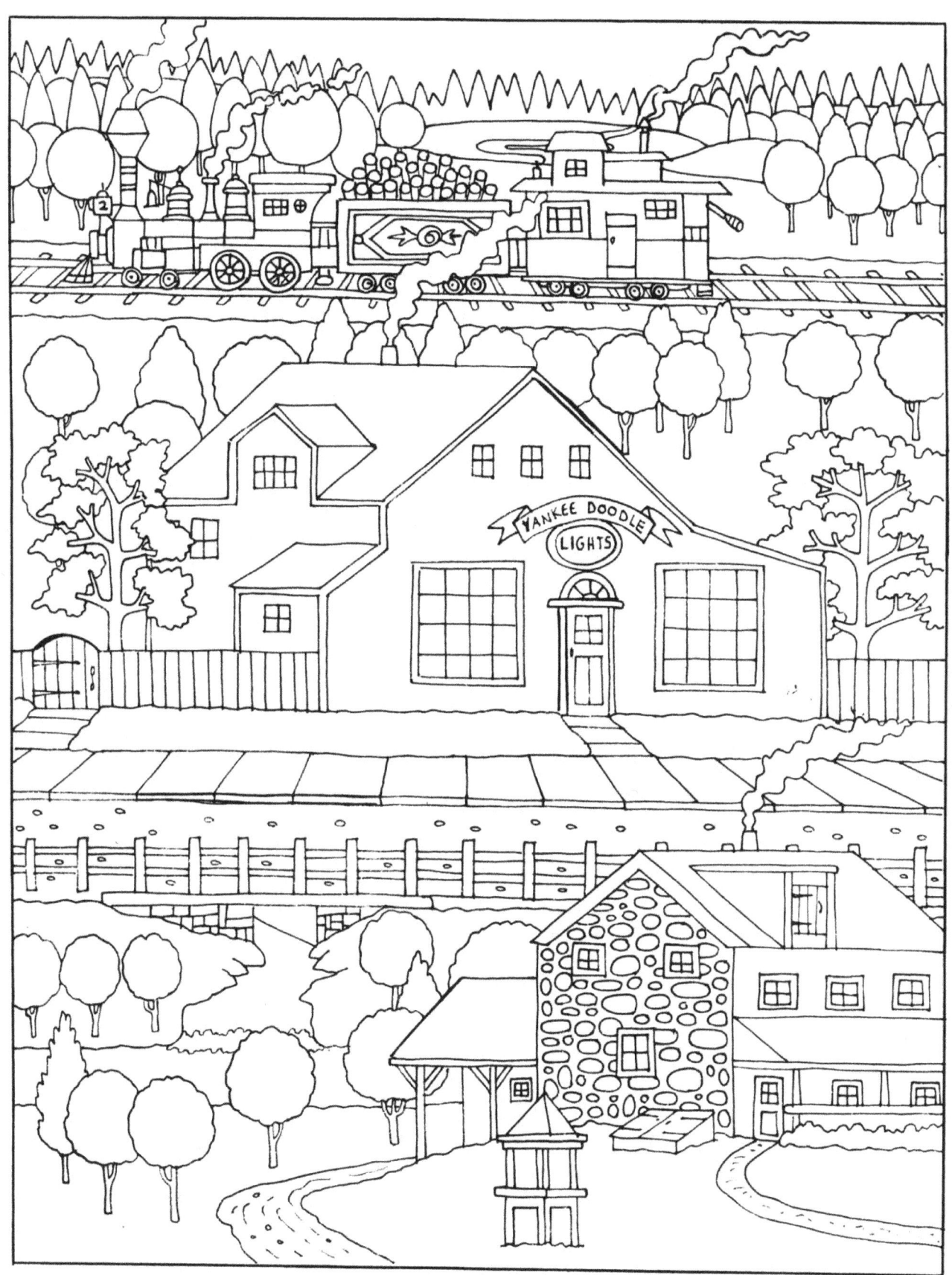

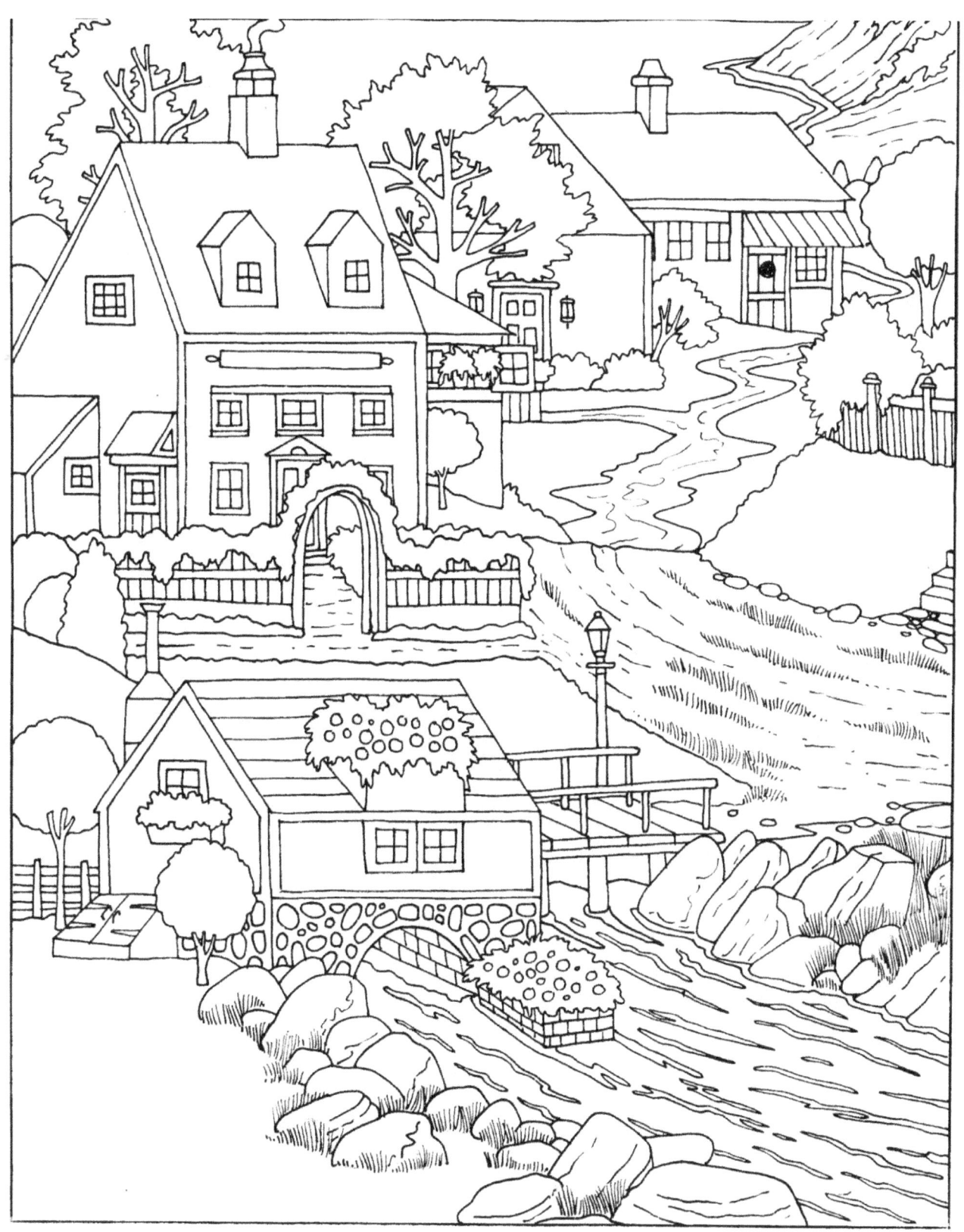

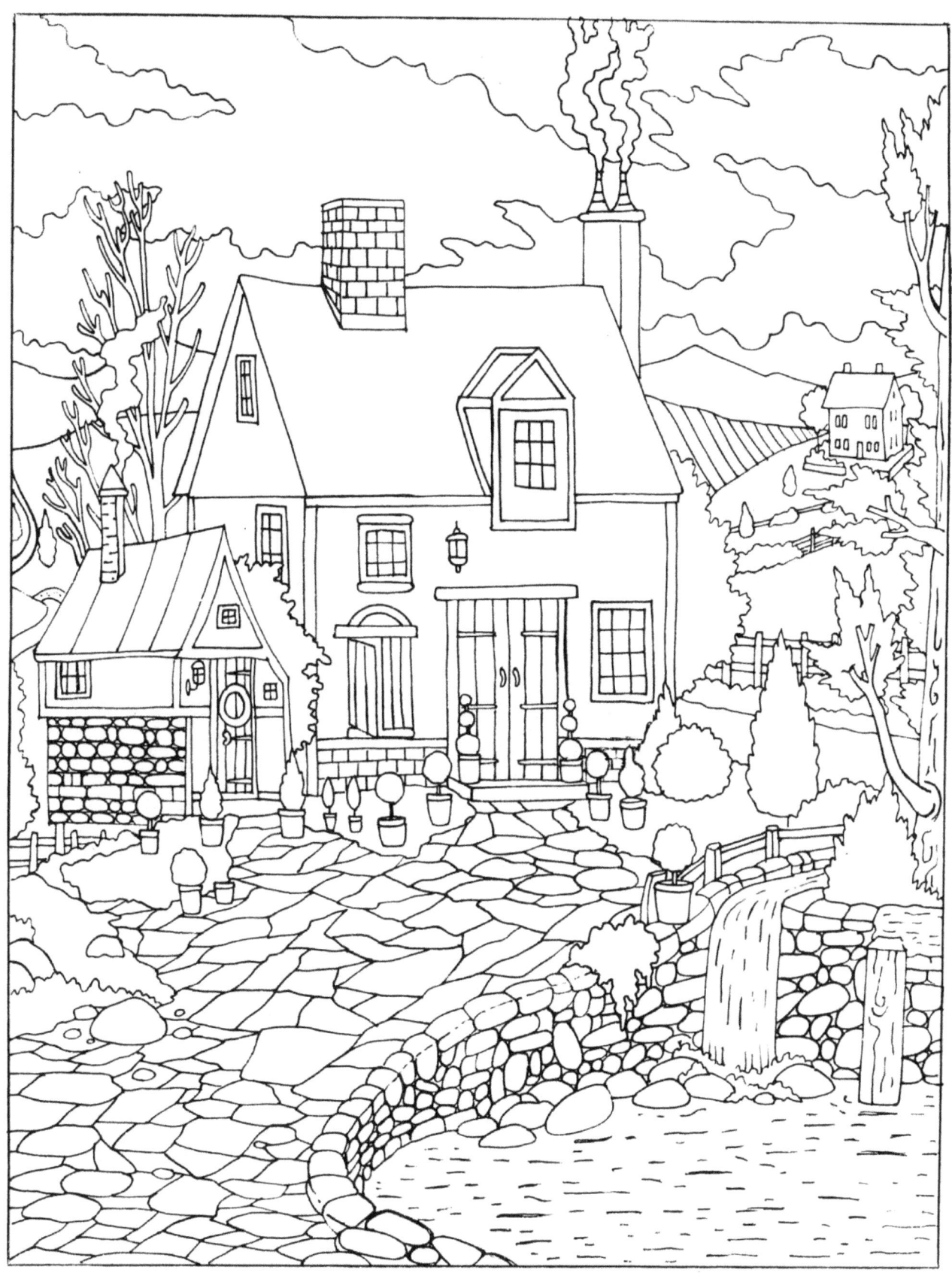

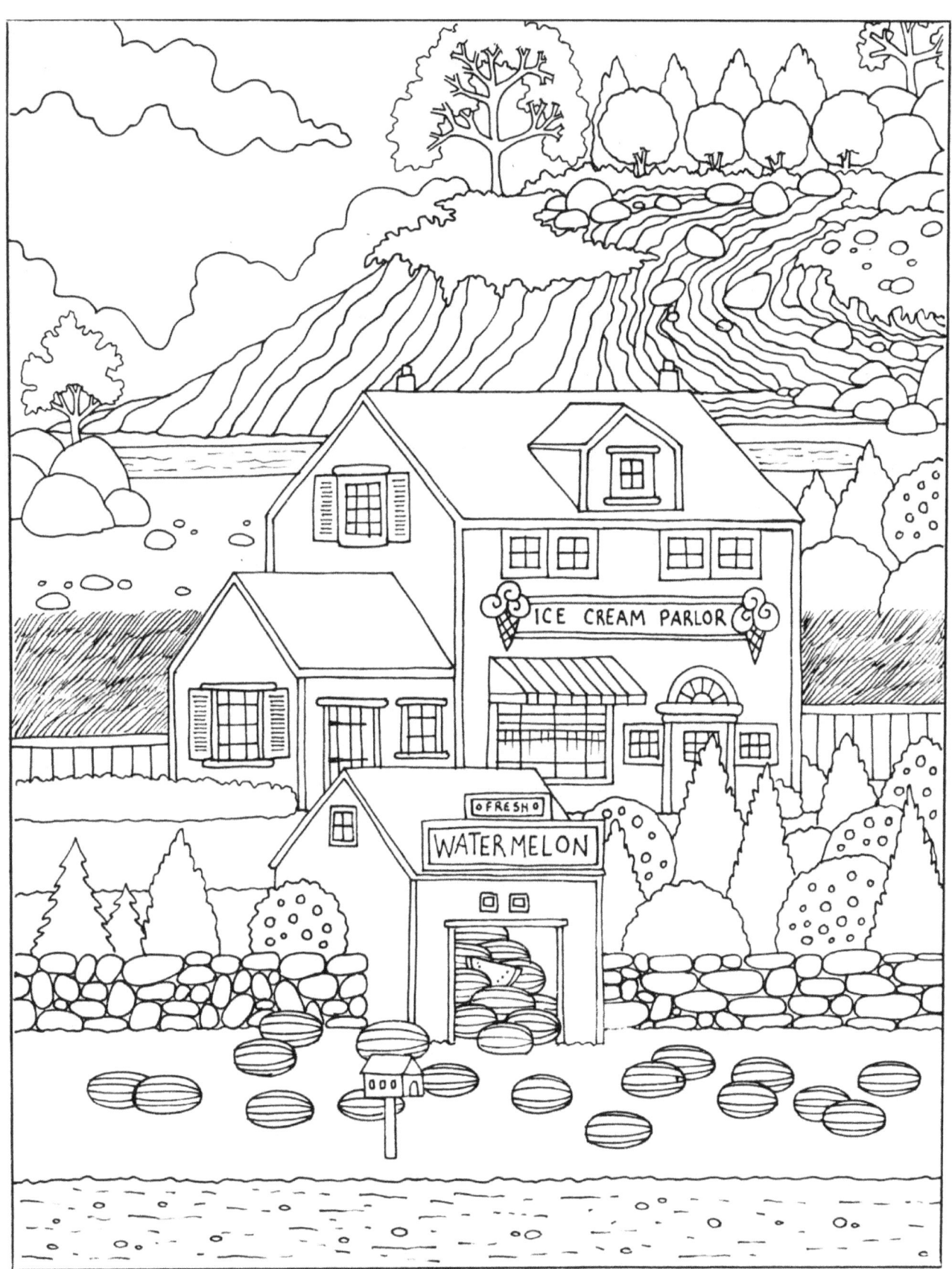

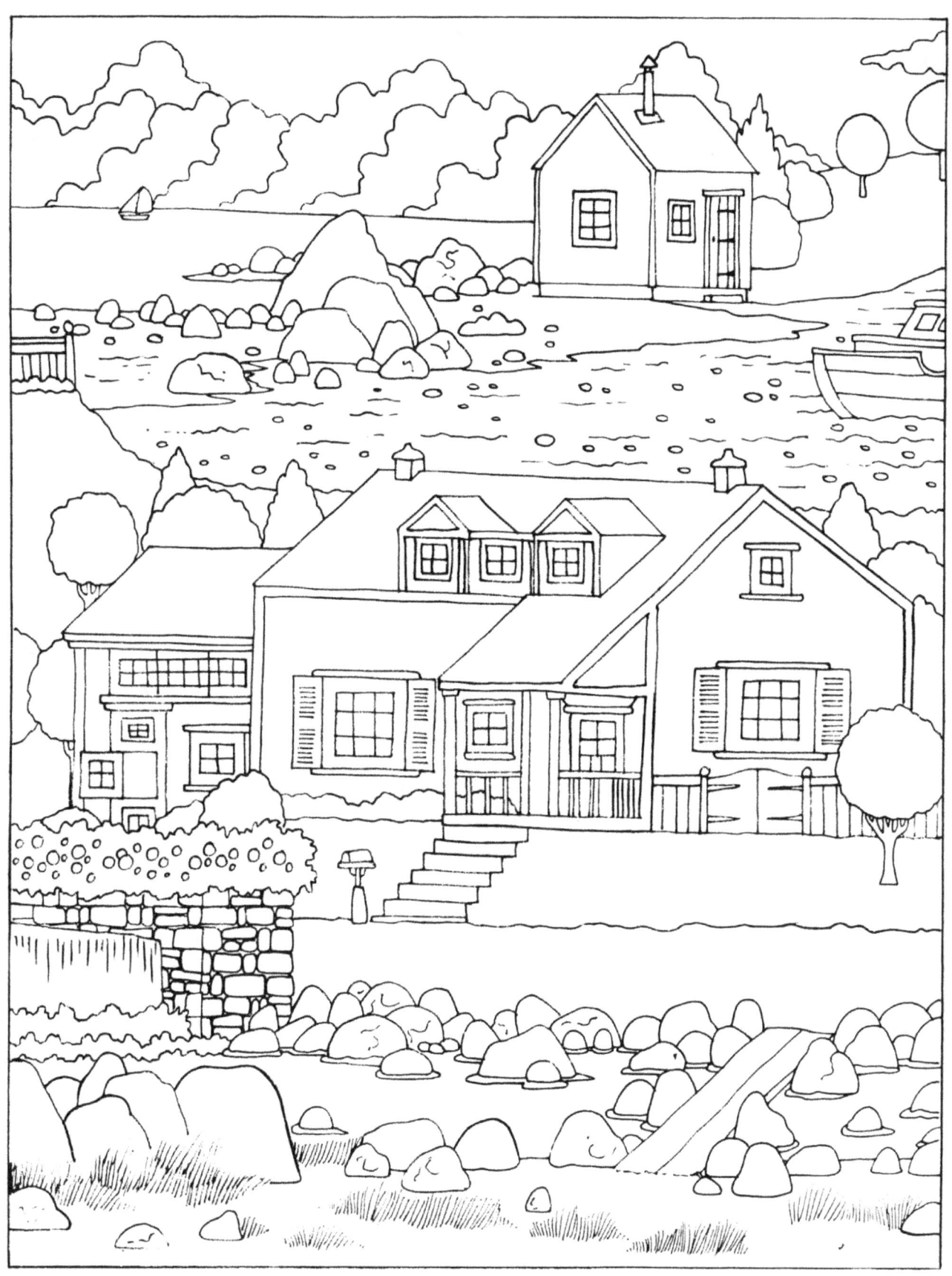

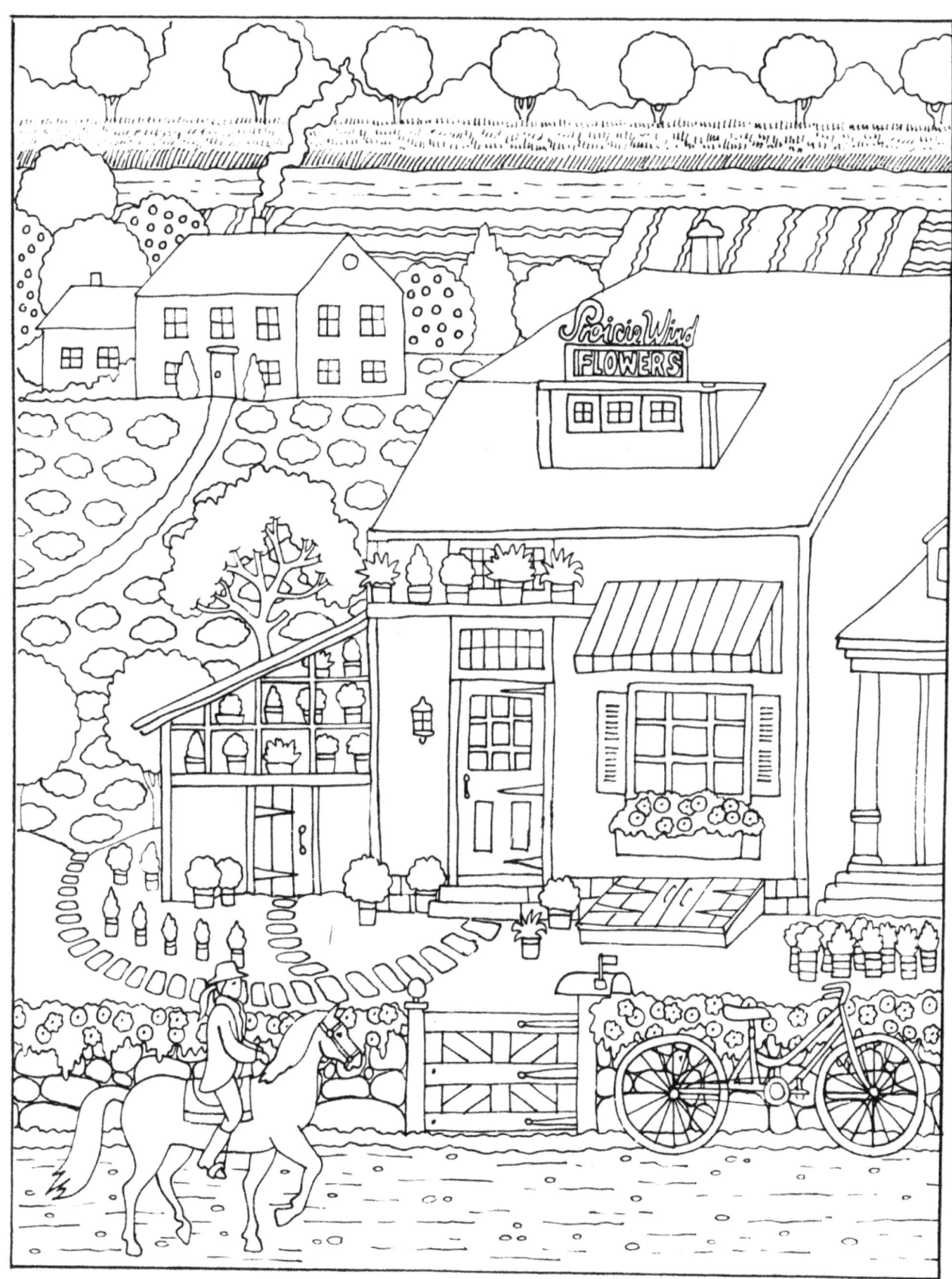

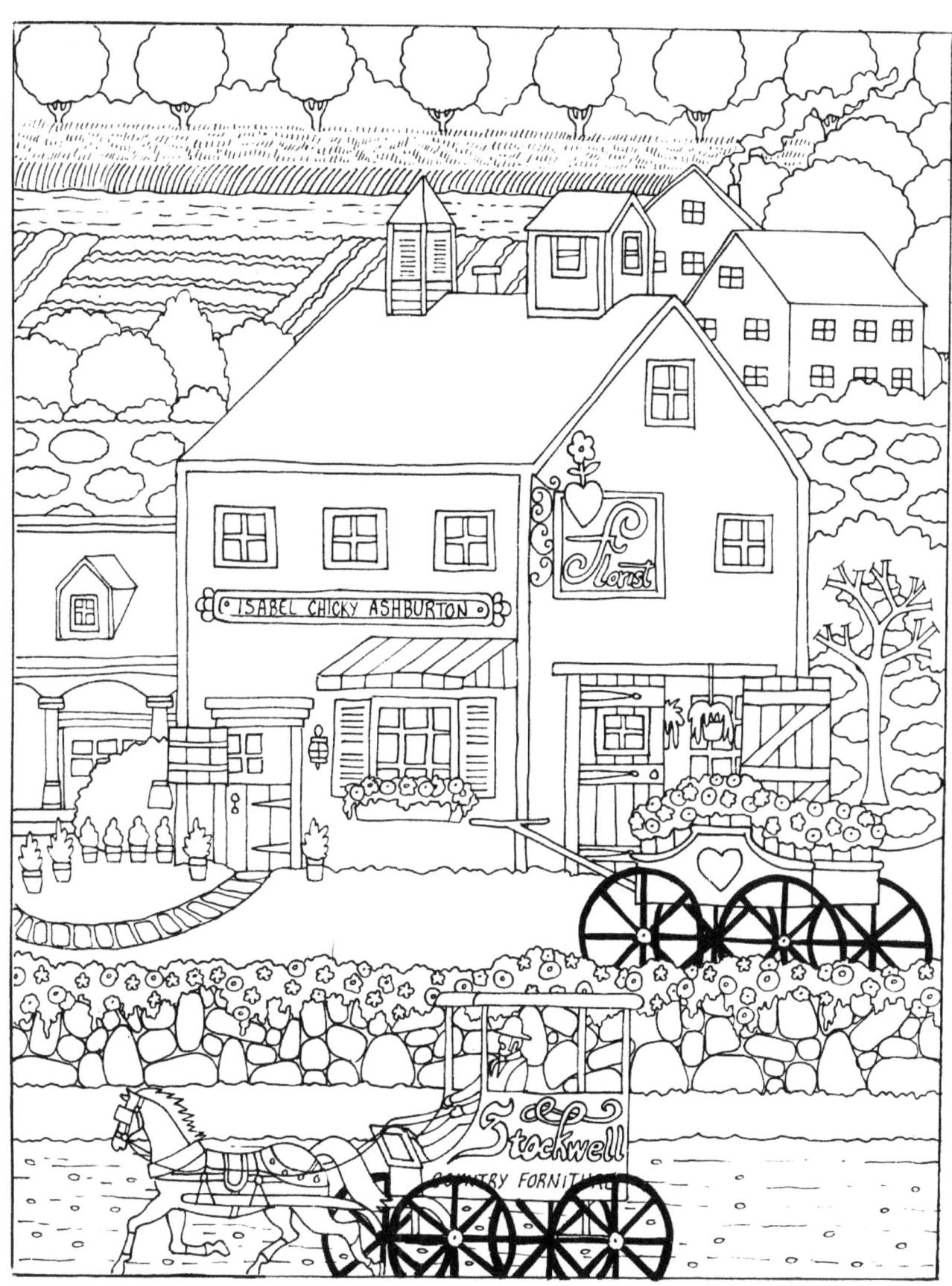

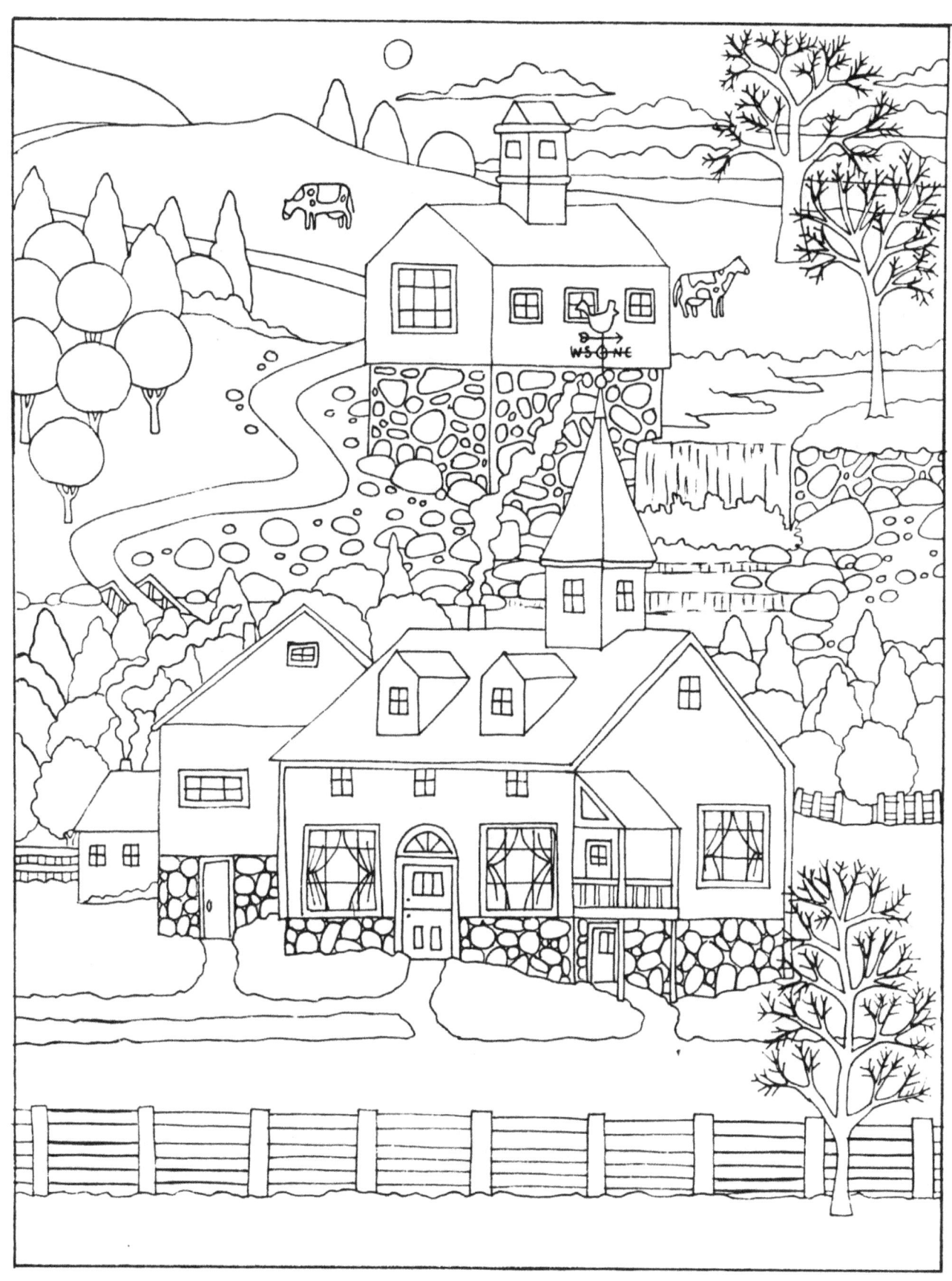

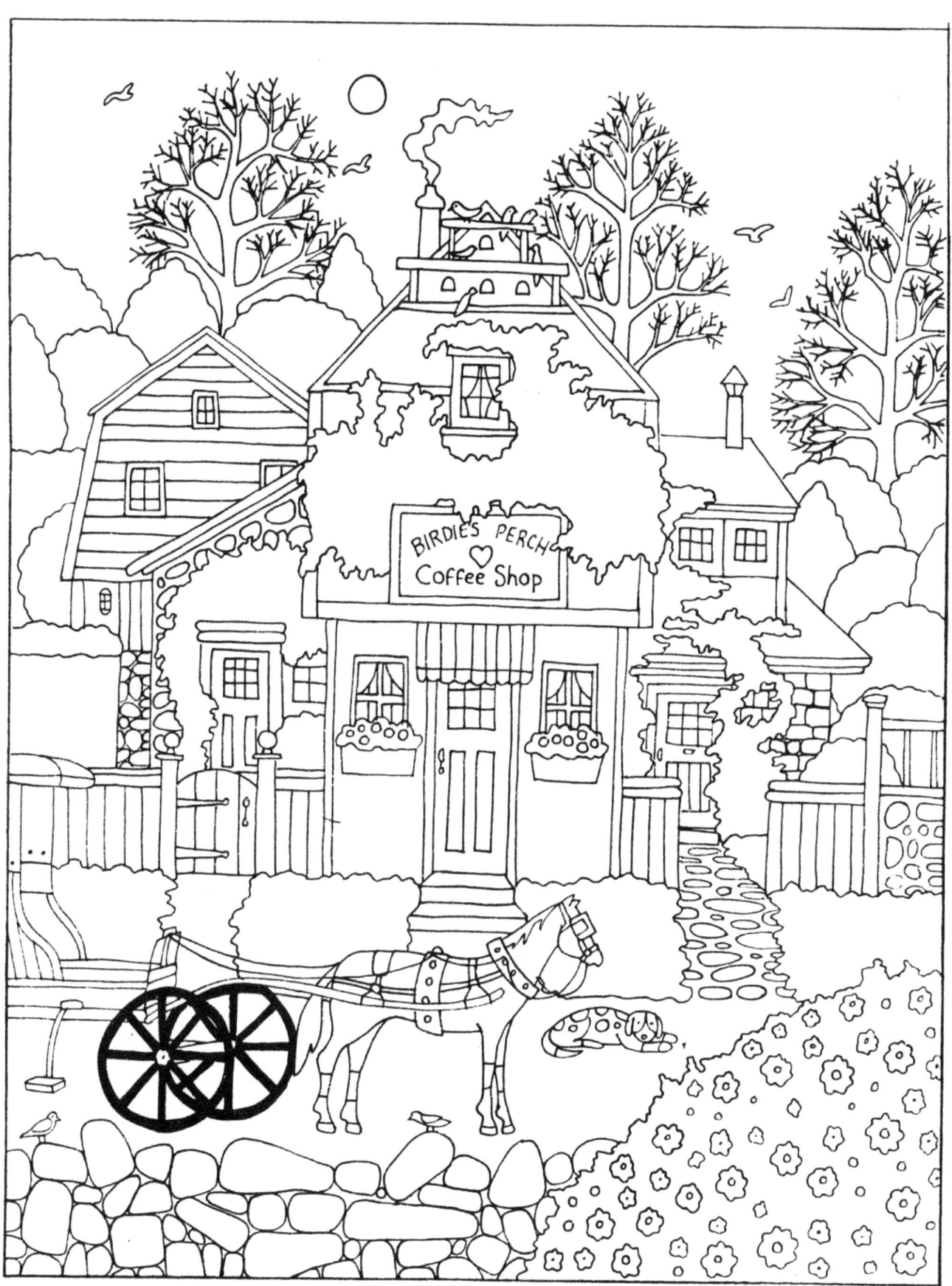

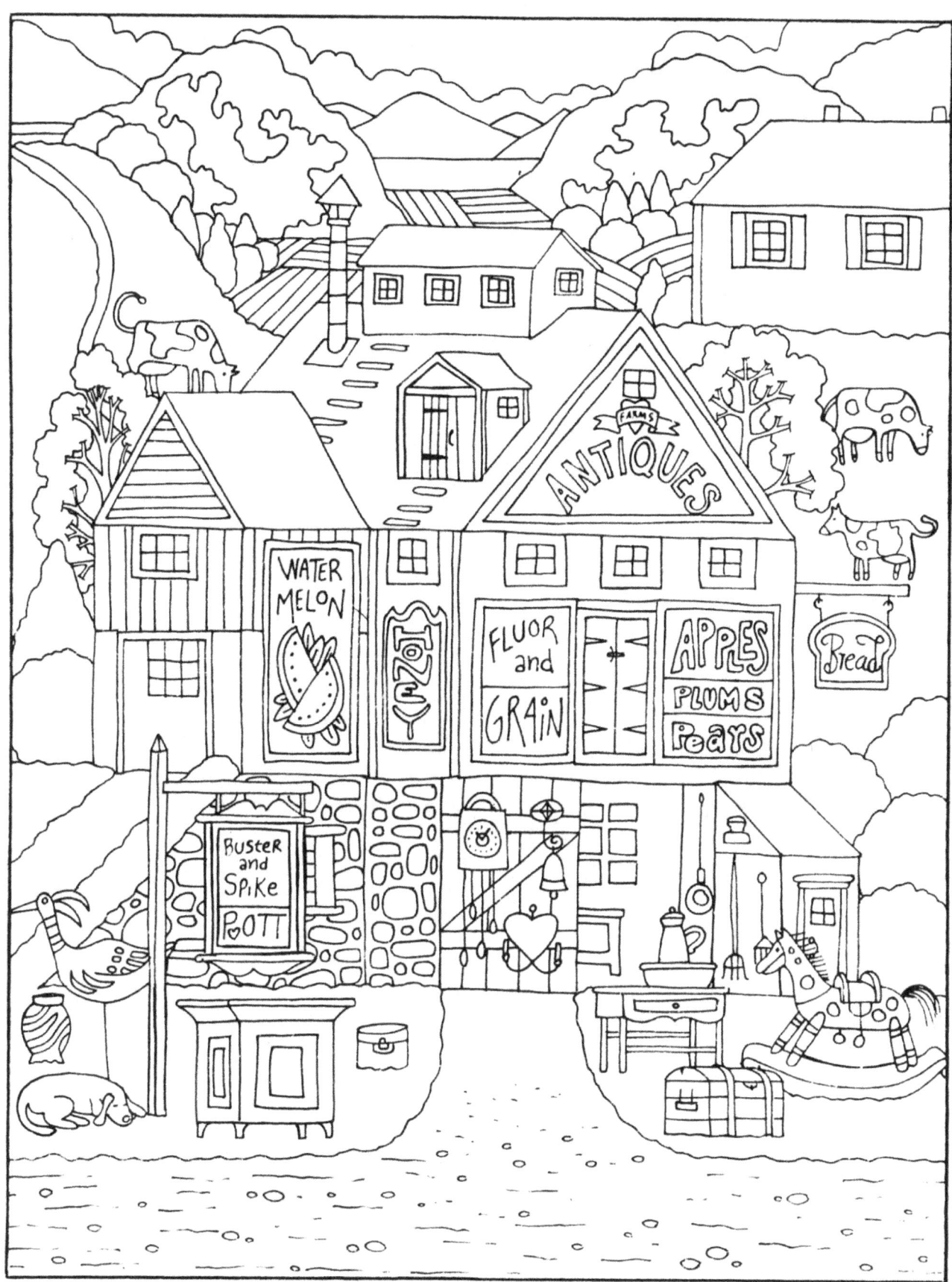

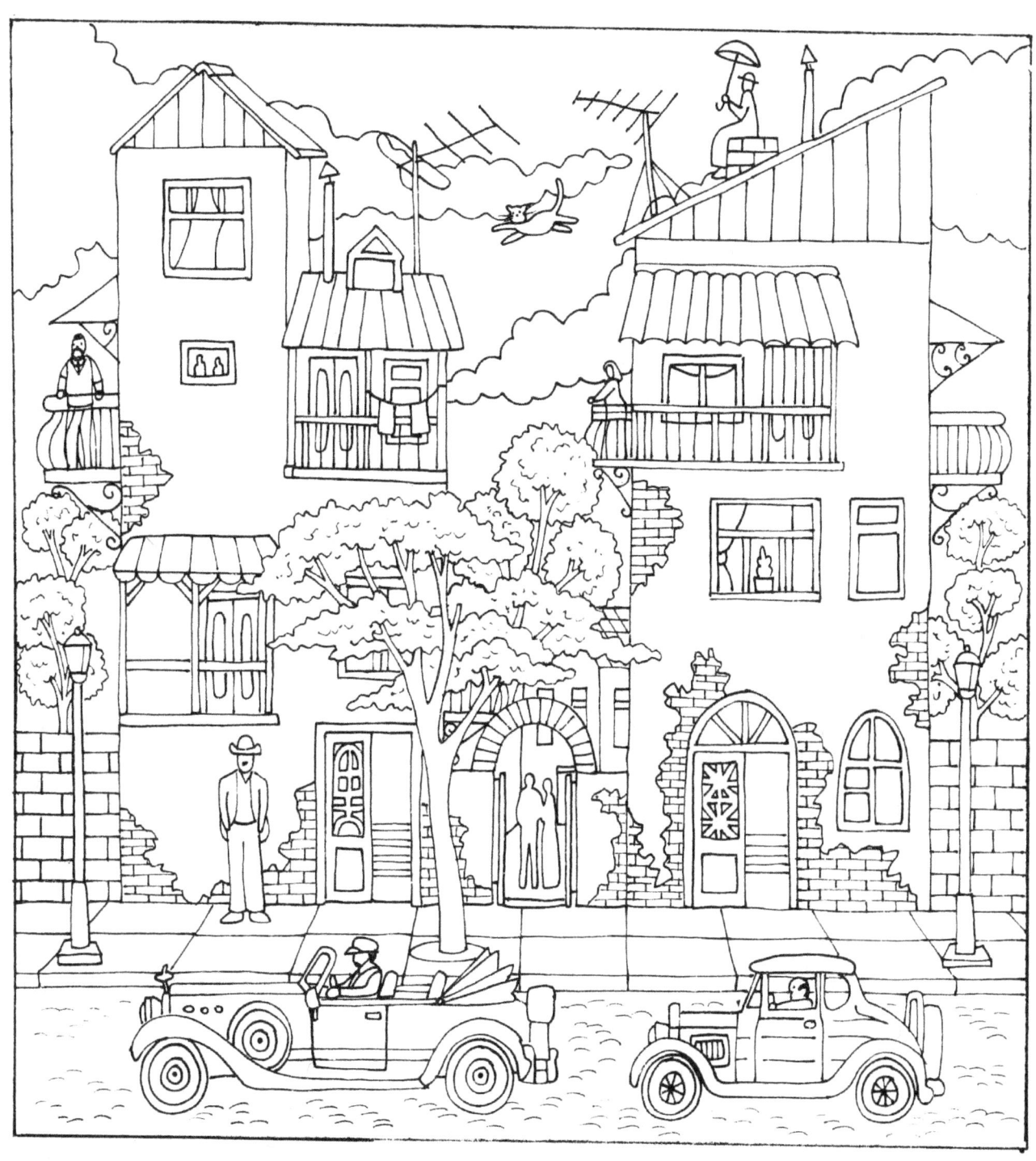

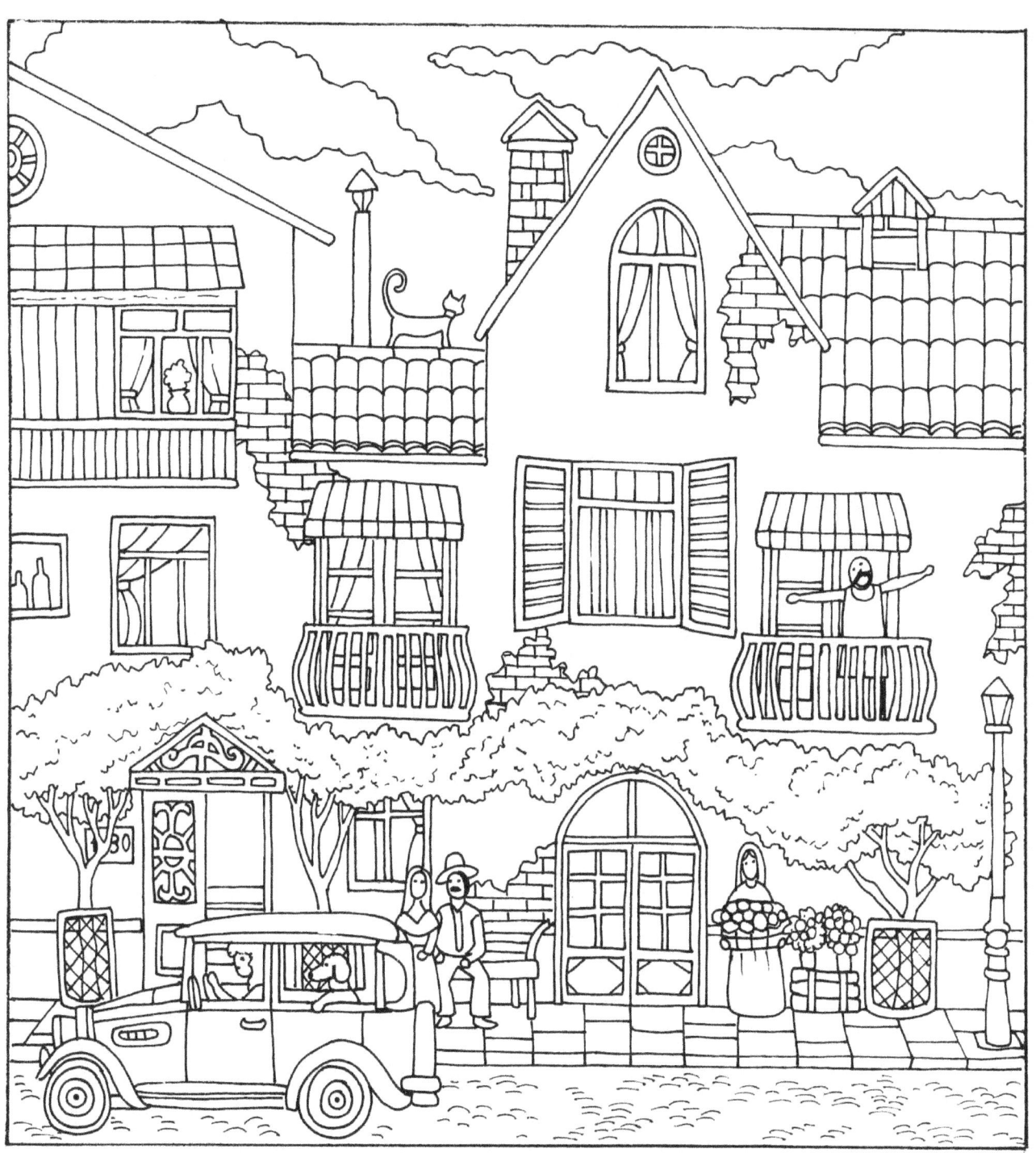